So many times in this world you'll hear people say,

"I hate this,

and I hate that!"

each and every day.

They seem to hate all kinds of
things. It really makes no sense!

Hate takes too much energy;
it all seems so intense.

"I hate cheese!"

"I hate cats!"

"I hate rain!"

"I hate rats!"

WAIT! WAIT! DON'T SAY HATE!

Don't use that word at all.
There's no reason to feel hate; it's pointless after all!

Cheese makes food delicious.
Cats love to purr and play.
Rain brings beauty to our world,
and rats - well, they're ok.

Rats may have long whiskers, beady eyes, and scary teeth, but they just like to roam around and look for yummy treats.

Sometimes you hear hate when you're at home or at the shops. Sometimes you hear hate when you are at the school bus stop.

Wait! Wait! Don't say hate, especially at school. If you use this awful word, you'll break a golden rule.

"I hate homework!"
"I hate chores!"
"I hate crowds in the stores!"

Wait! Wait! Don't say hate!

Homework makes you smarter
so your future will be bright.
Chores make you responsible,
and crowds – well they're all right.

Sometimes hate is in the classroom
or you hear it in the hall.
You hear it when you're having lunch
or trying to play ball.

Wait! Wait! Don't say hate!

A classroom is for learning
all the things we need each day.
A playground is for fun
and a hall will lead the way.

"I hate teachers!"
"I hate soup!"
"I hate birds when they poop!"

Wait! Wait! Don't say hate!

Soup will keep us warm on a cold and gloomy day.
Birds don't have a potty, so it's the only way.
Teachers may be stern and strict,
but really, they're ok.

Teachers help us when we're hurt
and make us happy when we're sad.
They teach us how to read and write.
Now how can that be bad?

Hate will never be our friend; it only makes us mad!
It zaps up all the energy we ever really had!

"I hate Veggies!"

"I hate spiders!

"I hate oatmeal and apple cider!"

Wait! Wait! Don't say hate!

Veggies and some oatmeal help you grow
stronger every day.
Apple cider's not for everyone,
and spiders - they're ok.

See, spiders like to eat the bugs that crawl and fly
around. If we didn't have the spiders, the bugs would
rule our town.

Cake Shop

CITY LIBRARY

POST OFFICE

MAIL

Sometimes you hear hate in the kitchen, a happy place for food. But it is just a kitchen. There's no need to be so rude!

"I hate pickles!"
"I hate eggs!"
"I hate cabinets too tall for my legs!"

Wait! Wait! Don't say hate!

Pickles are just cucumbers
that had to change their way.
Eggs have lots of protein,
and well, cabinets - they're ok.

Cabinets are for storing stuff that need a place to stay. If cabinets are too tall for you, let your parents show the way.

Hate can be heard everywhere. It can come as a surprise, on the ground, on your hands, or right before your eyes!

"I hate ants and messy glue!"

GLUE

"I hate baths and tying shoes!"

Wait! Wait! Don't say hate!

Glue holds things together; baths keep us clean each day.

Tying shoes keeps us safe, and ants - well they're ok.

See, ants are very strong and can carry lots of weight. They carry leaves and bugs home so they can fill their families' plates.

Sometimes hate is on the
beach and in the city park.
Hate can even follow us
when we are in the dark.

Wait! Wait! Don't say hate!

Beaches are so fun on a bright and sunny day.
Parks have swings and slides,
and the dark - well it's ok.

See, darkness lets the moon shine and gives the sun a rest.

It lets you get a good night's sleep so you can be your best!

"I hate dentists!"

"I hate clowns!"

"I hate seeing my friends frown!"

Wait! Wait! Don't say hate!

Dentists help protect our teeth so they don't have decay.

Friends sometimes wear a frown when they have a bad day, and clowns can look so scary, but really, they're ok.

Clowns will honk their horns; they juggle and they dance. So don't hate funny clowns; please give them a chance.

Clowns just want to make us laugh and bring a huge, huge smile. A big red nose and giant shoes are just their silly style.

Sometimes hate lives in our head and can travel to our toes. Our feelings get mixed and confused when hate runs the shows. So kick the hate word from your head, and drag it to a close.

BYE BYE HATE!

HATE

"Hate" can be heard everywhere; it really can be sad. It only takes your energy and makes you very mad.

There is no reason to feel hate no matter where you are - in the bus, at your school, or even in the car!

Everything is special, no matter near or far - different and unique just like each shining star!

So let us love all things from the largest to the small.
Love brings kindness, joy, and smiles.
It's the best after all!

Love your friends and your teachers; love the spider on the wall.
Love the cheese in your sandwich and the noise in the hall.

Love takes no energy; it flows as gently as a stream.
And a world filled with love is like the perfect dream!

Darlene Desbrow

Danielle Morton

Friends for over thirty years, Danielle Morton and Darlene Desbrow often discussed collaborating on a children's book. As educators in Orange County, California, Ms. Morton teaches at the elementary level and Dr. Desbrow is an adjunct professor of education and a middle school English Language Arts teacher.

Both authors are passionate about literature that provides children with valuable skills for becoming productive, kind, and compassionate human beings. Bringing the message of this book to life has been a dream come true for Danielle and Darlene, and they hope *Wait! Wait! Don't Say Hate!* will touch the lives of those who read it and inspire its readers to spread kindness and love throughout the world.

Illustrator Anna Fox

Anna Fox is a graphic artist and illustrator in Pittsburgh, PA. She worked as an in-house graphic designer for a balloon and gift box company before launching her freelance illustration career. She has a passion for art and loves spreading joy through her creativity. Illustrating *Wait! Wait! Don't Say Hate!* was a true pleasure for her, and she is honored to be a part of sharing Darlene and Danielle's message of love and kindness.